C000132755

BRE

THE TANGIBLE

BENEFITS

THE UK LEAVES THE EU

DAVID C REISS

&

SAM A ALAN

Clean break books

In memoriam membrum status XXVIII

Dedication

This book is dedicated to the chief architects and principles who campaigned to leave the European Union. Without them, this book would not have come to fruition.

About the Authors

David C. Reiss was born in 1949.

His professional life has led him to travel extensively around the world and he has observed many different cultures and societies first hand. Now retired, he has been a keen observer of politics both at home and abroad all his life. His contributions to this book are based largely on direct experience and a detailed observation of the situation in which the UK finds itself. He has neither direct political affiliations nor any involvement with any organisations; but remains a lay observer to events.

Sam A. Alan is a specialist in international services and trade, with over twenty-five years' experience gained in the hospitality, information technology and automotive sectors. He has a special interest on the effects policies of a post-Brexit United Kingdom will have on trade and services, and the wider impact this will have on UK society. He considers himself apolitical and his contributions to this book are from a neutral viewpoint.

Disclaimer

The views and opinions in this book are those of the authors and do not reflect the official policy or position of any political party or organisation. Examples of analysis performed within this book are only examples. They should not be utilised in real-world analytic products as they are based only on very limited and dated open source information.

Brexit – The Tangible Benefits

Contents

Foreword

This book is dedicated to all those who so tirelessly campaigned for a referendum on the UK's membership of the European Union over several decades.

The authors acknowledge that during the referendum campaign, both sides ("Leave" and "Remain") were somewhat negligent in their presentation of the facts. This book is an attempt to address that; and to present an objective view of the current situation.

No democratic decision can ever be perfect and the nature of democracy is such that some will be disappointed by the results of any vote.

Nevertheless, all the citizens of the country will be affected by the outcome of the vote. Whether or not they participated or voted against the final decision.

Leaving the EU will substantially change many aspects of life in the UK for its citizens, both at home and when it comes to overseas travel.

Businesses will adapt many of their working practices to the changed environment.

Consumers will find that the products available in shops and supermarkets will be affected by the fact that the UK is no longer a member of the EU.

Leaving the EU will be the single most important change to life in the UK since the end of WWII.

Following deep and extensive research, the book outlines the advantages of the UK's democratic decision to terminate its membership of the European Union.

Economy

This section outlines the tangible benefits of Brexit to various parts of the Economy

"A Clean-Break Brexit can also shape the future of our economy. It will give us the freedom to shape our future by taking immediate control of our own money" – The Brexit Party Contract

Banks – National & International

Thanks to Brexit, your Pound Sterling will remain in your UK bank. It may however not be accepted at any International banks. But this way, it is being kept British.

Turn page for more benefits >>>>

Income Tax

Your income tax will remain in the coffers of the British government. Thanks to Brexit, the Government will be able to decide where to spend this money.

Turn page for more benefits >>>>

VAT

The EU determines lower and upper limits of VAT. Thanks to Brexit, these limits will no longer be applicable, and the UK Treasury will be able to determine VAT and other consumer tax rates as it wishes.

Turn page for more benefits >>>>

Foreign Exchange

The Lisbon Treaty Article 142:- Member States must treat exchange rate policy as a matter of common interest

Thanks to Brexit, and similar to recent China monetary policy, the UK will be able to devalue its currency in order to boost cheap exports, shrink trade deficits and reduce sovereign debt burdens. Refer to Chapter Trade for further details.

Turn page for more benefits >>>>

Inflation

Thanks to Brexit, inflation could decrease or increase as the UK government will be free to exercise monetary policy as it decides. This will be dependent on Foreign Exchange and Interest Rates outlined in this section.

Turn page for more benefits >>>>

nterest rates

Thanks to Brexit, interest rates could decrease or increase as the UK government will be free to exercise monetary policy as it decides. This will be dependent on Foreign Exchange and Inflation outlined in this section.

Turn page for more benefits >>>>

Jobs

From the Conservative Party Website:-

"With every home we make, every mile of full fibre broadband we lay, with every flood-defending culvert we dig, with every railway station, hospital or school we build, we will of course be helping to create thousands of high-paid high-skilled jobs…a new dynamic commercial spirit to make the most of UK breakthroughs, so that British ideas produce new British industries and British jobs"

This is of course subject to British citizens wanting to and being qualified to work in the fields alluded to.

Turn page for more benefits >>>>

Society

This section outlines the beneficial effects of Brexit on UK society

Turn page for more benefits >>>>

Jobs

From the Conservative Party Website:-

"With every home we make, every mile of full fibre broadband we lay, with every flood-defending culvert we dig, with every railway station, hospital or school we build, we will of course be helping to create thousands of high-paid high-skilled jobs...a new dynamic commercial spirit to make the most of UK breakthroughs, so that British ideas produce new British industries and British jobs"

This is of course subject to British citizens wanting to and being qualified to work in the fields alluded to.

Turn page for more benefits >>>>

Welfare

Thanks to Brexit, the UK government will be in control of pensions and welfare for some of its residents. Those citizens residing in an EU country will not receive the same benefits of Benefits as those living in the UK, thus lowering the UK's welfare burden.

Turn page for more benefits >>>>

Culture

Thanks to Brexit, a weakening Pound will mean we will experience an increase in UK tourism and a potential increase in collaboration with countries outside the EU.

Turn page for more benefits >>>>

Consumer activity

Thanks to Brexit, UK consumers will be able to buy more British products, as a result of having less access to foreign products. Prices may increase due to an uncompetitive market.

Turn page for more benefits >>>>

Politics

Thanks to Brexit, the Government will now have more control. The Civil Service (unelected bureaucrats), and much of Parliament, will be controlled by the Government, as will the citizens of the UK.

Turn page for more benefits >>>>

Freedom of speech

EU Charter of Fundamental Rights Article 11:- "Everyone has the right of freedom of expression...without interference by public authority and regardless of frontiers."

Thanks to Brexit, the UK Government will be able to prevent publications beyond its borders being published in the UK.

Charles Koch Institute:- "...there is hope that when the UK is no longer a member of the EU, it will be able to maintain its historically robust tradition of freedom of expression – a tradition it shares with the United States"

Turn page for more benefits >>>>

Human Rights

Thanks to Brexit, the UK's fundamental rights will no longer be subject to the constitutional traditions common to EU member states.

Turn page for more benefits >>>>

Policing

Thanks to Brexit, the British Police force will no longer be forced to liaise with their counterparts in EU member states.

Turn page for more benefits >>>>

Defence

Thanks to Brexit, the UK will not be forced to join an EU defence force, whenever one is formed.

Turn page for more benefits >>>>

Immigration and Asylum

Thanks to Brexit, the UK will now be able to create its own immigration policies. It will not be bound by EU regulations, such as those allowing a member state to return an asylum seeker to their first point of entry into the EU.

Turn page for more benefits >>>>

Culture

This section outlines the beneficial effects of Brexit on UK culture

"Leavers, by contrast, feel that these institutions have come to be dominated by a left-liberal cultural establishment that looks down on them and sells the country short. They accuse the BBC of having a left-wing bias. They believe that universities serve to indoctrinate their children. And though they are confident that their country could manage on its own, they have grown convinced that most politicians are too timid to help it regain its past grandeur."

The Atlantic

Turn page for more benefits >>>>

Jobs

From the Conservative Party Website:-

"With every home we make, every mile of full fibre broadband we lay, with every flood-defending culvert we dig, with every railway station, hospital or school we build, we will of course be helping to create thousands of high-paid high-skilled jobs...a new dynamic commercial spirit to make the most of UK breakthroughs, so that British ideas produce new British industries and British jobs"

This is of course subject to British citizens wanting to and being qualified to work in the fields alluded to.

Turn page for more benefits >>>>

Film

Thanks to Brexit, filmmakers will be able to make full use of UK locations for their films. Where an appropriate location cannot be found, filmmakers will be able to utilise the talents of any CGI companies operating in the UK.

Turn page for more benefits >>>>

Television

Thanks to Brexit, broadcasting companies have the choice of only taking out a UK broadcasting licence to air their programmes solely in the UK. They can of course pay extra by also taking out a European broadcasting licence to continue airing programmes throughout the EU.

Turn page for more benefits >>>>

Radio

Thanks to Brexit, broadcasting companies have the choice of only taking out a UK broadcasting licence to air their programmes solely in the UK. They can of course pay extra by also taking out a European broadcasting licence to continue airing programmes throughout the EU.

Turn page for more benefits >>>>

Theatre

Bertolt Brecht:- "In the dark times, will there also be singing? Yes, there will also be singing. About the dark times."

Thanks to Brexit, UK theatre will focus efforts on entertaining UK audiences with UK actors.

Turn page for more benefits >>>>

Music

Thanks to Brexit, European funding of UK music projects will be cut. However, the U.K. Government could increase this funding should it wish to do so.

Turn page for more benefits >>>>

port

Clubs may be unable to attract European sports stars into their teams. Thanks to Brexit, home grown talent will have a chance to shine.

Turn page for more benefits >>>>

Literature

Thanks to Brexit, this book was able to come to fruition. Others will follow, in both the speculative and reflective genres.

Turn page for more benefits >>>>

Transport and Travel

This section outlines the beneficial effects of Brexit on UK transport and travel

"Not content with having wasted the best part of £14m on the government's first-ever roll-on, roll-off pizza delivery service – all toppings guaranteed to be ferry free, the transport secretary has now spent more than £50k on failing to organise a lorry jam in Kent."

John Crace writing in the Guardian

Turn page for more benefits >>>>

Jobs

From the Conservative Party Website:-

"With every home we make, every mile of full fibre broadband we lay, with every flood-defending culvert we dig, with every railway station, hospital or school we build, we will of course be helping to create thousands of high-paid high-skilled jobs...a new dynamic commercial spirit to make the most of UK breakthroughs, so that British ideas produce new British industries and British jobs"

This is of course subject to British citizens wanting to and being qualified to work in the fields alluded to.

Turn page for more benefits >>>>

Private vehicle manufacture and maintenance

Tariffs could be applied to vehicles and their component parts made outside the UK. Thanks to Brexit, we could see a heyday of UK motor manufacturing and a potential revival of companies popular in the 1970s such as British Leyland and Austin.

Turn page for more benefits >>>>

Public Transport

Thanks to Brexit, if European subsidised transport companies are no longer able to run British transport franchises, the profits that these franchises make will remain in the UK.

Turn page for more benefits >>>>

Logistics

Thanks to Brexit, road hauliers will be able to benefit from extended rest periods during their haulage activities between the UK and the EU and Northern Ireland. The Government is currently creating a rest area for drivers.

Turn page for more benefits >>>>

Aviation

Thanks to Brexit, the restrictions and consequent visas necessary for UK citizens travelling to European destinations will reduce the carbon footprint significantly. The carbon footprint will be rebalanced by more UK citizens driving to holiday destinations in the UK.

Turn page for more benefits >>>>

isas

hanks to Brexit, UK citizens travelling to European destinations will ow have a record in their passports to reminisce over their visits. At oints of entry, they will also have the advantage of not having to ueue in the same lines as EU citizens.

Turn page for more benefits >>>>

Hotels and hospitality

Thanks to Brexit, the reduction in overseas holiday making will be a boon for British hotels and hospitality. See also Jobs, Trade, Foreign Exchange, Inflation and Transport.

Turn page for more benefits >>>>

Customs

Thanks to Brexit, thousands of jobs will be created in the customs sector, including Border Force and customs agents. There will also be an increase in tax revenue for the Exchequer. See also Logistics and Jobs.

Turn page for more benefits >>>>

Passports

Thanks to Brexit, UK citizens will feel they are getting value for money from their passport as it fills up with stamps from EU countries they choose to visit. UK citizens will also be able to obtain new passport more frequently as the pages will be used more often.

Turn page for more benefits >>>>

nsurance

hanks to Brexit, every UK citizen travelling to the EU will now have
o purchase some form of travel insurance to replace the European
Health Insurance Card. UK citizens falling ill whilst on holiday in an EU
ountry will now have the choice of paying for either state or private
medical healthcare and claiming the money back from their travel
nsurance company, subject to any excesses applied.

Turn page for more benefits >>>>

Trade

This section outlines the beneficial effects of Brexit on UK trade

"Let's recall the benefits of 'No Deal' – a WTO-based Brexit could yield the UK £80 billion per year"

Brexit Central

Turn page for more benefits >>>>

obs

rom the Conservative Party Website:-

"With every home we make, every mile of full fibre broadband we ay, with every flood-defending culvert we dig, with every railway tation, hospital or school we build, we will of course be helping to reate thousands of high-paid high-skilled jobs...a new dynamic ommercial spirit to make the most of UK breakthroughs, so that ritish ideas produce new British industries and British jobs"

his is of course subject to British citizens wanting to and being ualified to work in the fields alluded to.

Turn page for more benefits >>>>

Agriculture

Thanks to Brexit, UK citizens will potentially be able to purchase more home grown produce, subject to seasonable availability.

Turn page for more benefits >>>>

Manufacturing

Thanks to Brexit, there will be more flexibility for manufacturing companies as they won't be tied to current safety and economic regulations in place. This is of course subject to the UK Government deregulating the UK manufacturing sector.

Turn page for more benefits >>>>

Research

Researchers in the UK will no longer have access to funding from the EU and may no longer be able to collaborate with researchers based in the EU. Thanks to Brexit, the UK Government will be able to fund UK research directly from the public purse and encourage home grown talent.

Turn page for more benefits >>>>

tandards

hanks to Brexit, the UK Government will be able to setup new egulations for product standards. These products will be tested in he UK for conformity to the new UK standards. Those nanufacturers wishing to sell their products to EU member states vill be free to have their products also tested by the relevant EU esting authority.

Turn page for more benefits >>>>

Services

In 2019, the UK enjoyed a surplus of £23 billion on trade in services to the EU. Thanks to Brexit, UK based service providing companies will be able to benefit from not requiring to adhere to EU standards to sell their services in the UK.

Turn page for more benefits >>>>

rade agreements

hanks to Brexit, the UK will be able to forge trade agreements with
ıe EU and all other countries around the world. The UK will have to
elinquish a small amount of sovereignty for each trade deal it
trikes.

Turn page for more benefits >>>>

Tariffs

Thanks to Brexit, the UK Government will be free to set tariffs on all imports to the UK, including those from EU member states. Like for like tariffs will be set by countries on any products they import from the UK. The price of imports and exports will therefore be dependent on UK Government policy.

Turn page for more benefits >>>>

Imports & Exports

Thanks to Brexit, all EU imports and exports will be subject to tariffs, customs checks and standards. UK manufacturing will have to increase production for UK consumers to compensate for any delays in importing goods from the EU.

Turn page for more benefits >>>>

Science & Medicine

This section outlines the beneficial effects of Brexit on Science and Medicine

A new single agency for the UK that includes health technology assessment could take on these challenges and create a model system equipped for real advances in regulatory science and making the UK an attractive site to launch new products. What is now needed is openness in discussion, boldness and political commitment.

Sir Alasdair Breckenridge writing in the Financial Times

Turn page for more benefits >>>>

obs

From the Conservative Party Website:-

With every home we make, every mile of full fibre broadband we lay, with every flood-defending culvert we dig, with every railway station, hospital or school we build, we will of course be helping to create thousands of high-paid high-skilled jobs...a new dynamic commercial spirit to make the most of UK breakthroughs, so that British ideas produce new British industries and British jobs"

This is of course subject to British citizens wanting to and being qualified to work in the fields alluded to.

Turn page for more benefits >>>>

Research

The UK Government will need to address all of the priority issues for the science community —funding, people, collaboration, regulation and facilities—as a coherent whole rather than a list of separate considerations. Thanks to Brexit, the UK Government will be able to replace EU funding for research with funding from the public purse.

Turn page for more benefits >>>>

Healthcare

Thanks to Brexit, the UK Government will be able to train more UK based nurses and doctors to replace those from the EU who have decided to return to their countries of origin. See Jobs.

Turn page for more benefits >>>>

Pharmaceuticals

Thanks to Brexit, the two major UK based pharmaceutical companies will be able to carry out more research and development in the UK. They may also be able to take over the roles of foreign pharmaceutical companies based in the UK due to regulatory standards, if their budgets allow. The Exchequer may see a rise in tax revenue should prices of medicines increase as a result.

Turn page for more benefits >>>>

erospace

he likes of Boeing and Airbus may remove investment and roduction from the UK. Thanks to Brexit, this will provide an pportunity for UK aerospace companies to create planes and pacecraft solely for the UK.

Turn page for more benefits >>>>

International cooperation

Thanks to Brexit, UK companies will be able to cooperate with countries all over the world. The UK will have to relinquish a small amount of sovereignty with each country it decided to cooperate with.

Turn page for more benefits >>>>

carbon neutrality

Thanks to Brexit, the UK Government will be able to improve on some EU policy approaches if it chooses to do so.

Turn page for more benefits >>>>

Education

Thanks to Brexit, universities should be able to provide more places for UK students. UK students will also have the opportunity to learn the local languages of any new trading partners the UK government engages with, for example Hindi, Jamaican Patois, Malagasy, Arabic and Hebrew.

Afterword

enefits of Brexit to the Ulster/Eire border: The authors have xamined the question and regretfully have been unable to come up 'ith any tangible benefit whatsoever.

hose elected to lead this country for the next four and a half years, ong with those rich enough to influence their policies, will not reap ny of the benefits alluded to in this book.

owever, all those who voted in the Referendum – as well as those ho didn't – will benefit equally from the items listed.

Timeline

1946: During a speech in Zurich in 1946, Winston Churchill spoke of the need to form a 'European Family' or a 'United States of Europe' to ensure peace and prosperity for Europe.

1972: For several years the debate ensued and both for economic and trade reasons, it was decided by the Heath Government to appl for membership. The European Communities Act 1972 was enacted on 17 October, and the UK's instrument of ratification was deposite the next day (18 October) letting the United Kingdom's membership of the EC come into effect on 1 January 1973.

1975: The debate continued, however, and in 1975 a UK referendur on continued membership of the EEC, the electorate voted 'Yes' by 67.2% to 32.8% to stay in Europe.

1975 to 2015: In the following decades, a group of dedicated politicians and others, campaigned tirelessly to have the results of the 1975 referendum overturned; and in the run up to the 2015 election, David Cameron promised in the manifesto that a referendum on the subject would be held if The Conservatives gained power. Which they did with a substantial majority.

2016: Consequently, in 2016 a referendum took place on the 23 June. The referendum resulted in 51.9% of the votes cast being in favour of leaving the EU.

2020: The UK formally left the EU on 31 January 2020

Printed in Great Britain
by Amazon